ANIMALSAURUS

INCREDIBLE CREATURES FROM PREHISTORIC AND MODERN TIMES

Tracey Turner

illustrated by Harriet Russell

BLOOMSBURY

NEW YORK LONDON OXFORD NEW DELHI SYDNEY

FOR TOBY BATTERSBY.
SORRY ABOUT THE BASILOSAURUS.

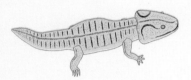

Text copyright © 2016 by Tracey Turner
Illustrations copyright © 2016 by Harriet Russell
Additional images all © Shutterstock

First published in Great Britain as *Animasaurus* in November 2016 by Bloomsbury Publishing Plc
Published in the United States of America in October 2017 by Bloomsbury Children's Books
www.bloomsbury.com

Bloomsbury is a registered trademark of Bloomsbury Publishing Plc

For information about permission to reproduce selections from this book, write to
Permissions, Bloomsbury Children's Books, 1385 Broadway, New York, New York 10018
Bloomsbury books may be purchased for business or promotional use. For information on bulk
purchases please contact Macmillan Corporate and Premium Sales Department at
specialmarkets@macmillan.com

Library of Congress Cataloging-in-Publication Data
Names: Turner, Tracey, author. | Russell, Harriet, illustrator.
Title: Animalsaurus / by Tracey Turner ; illustrated by Harriet Russell.
Description: New York : Bloomsbury, 2017.
Identifiers: LCCN 2017007109
ISBN 978-1-68119-544-5 (hardcover)
Subjects: LCSH: Animals, Fossil—Juvenile literature. | Extinct
animals—Juvenile literature.
Classification: LCC QE765 .T87 2017 | DDC 560—dc23
LC record available at https://lccn.loc.gov/2017007109

Printed in China by Leo Paper Products, Heshan, Guangdong
2 4 6 8 10 9 7 5 3 1

All papers used by Bloomsbury Publishing, Inc., are natural, recyclable products made from wood grown in well-managed forests.
The manufacturing processes conform to the environmental regulations of the country of origin.

INTRODUCTION

The world today is full of unusual and wonderful animals. Some are striped or spotted, some have trunks or horns, and some weigh 200 tons and have tongues as heavy as a rhino. But these amazing creatures are only a small fraction of all the animals that have ever lived—and some of them were really weird! Prepare to have your mind boggled, because we're about to meet . . .

- A monster guinea pig that weighed a ton
- Reptiles with wings
- Rodents with horns
- The most terrifying dinosaur of them all!

Read on to find out about incredible prehistoric beasts as well as the modern-day animals that share some of their amazing features.

Fantastic Fossils

We know about most of the amazing creatures in this book because of their fossils. A fossil is made when an animal dies and its body is covered in sand, mud, or something similar before other animals have had a chance to run (or swim) off with bits of it. Over thousands and thousands of years, the sand or mud becomes rock. Meanwhile, the animal's bones rot away inside the rock, and the spaces they leave become filled with minerals—like plaster poured into a mold. More time passes (maybe millions of years) before the rock is exposed for a lucky fossil-hunter to find.

Deep Freeze

There are other types of fossil too. For example, animals might be preserved if they are completely frozen in ice. Woolly mammoths and rhinos have been found in frozen ground, complete with skin and clumps of hair, tens of thousands of years after they died.

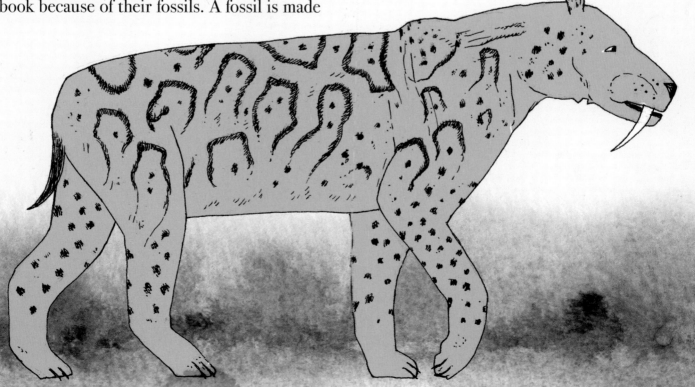

Prehistoric Contents

Prehistoric Plant-eaters

Prehistoric Sea creatures

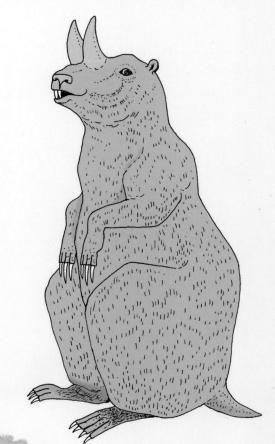

PREHISTORIC PREDATORS

PREHISTORIC CREEPY-CRAWLIES

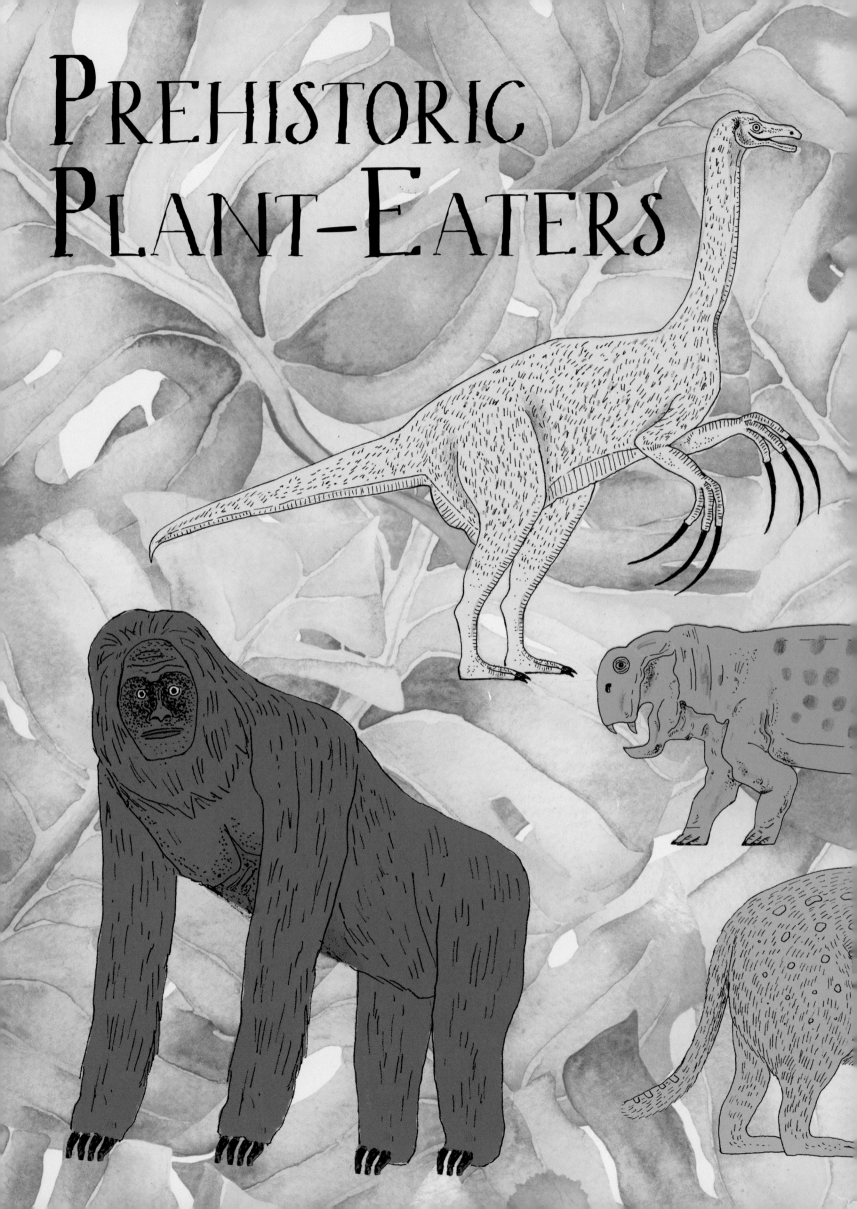

Prehistoric Plant-Eaters

Meet giant gorillas and monster guinea pigs, and uncover woolly rhinos preserved in the ice of the frozen north. These plant-eating beasts boasted strange-looking horns, claws three feet long, and giant chomping teeth . . .

WOOLLY RHINOCEROS

Ten thousand years ago, woolly rhinoceroses with three-foot-long horns roamed Asia and Europe. Their long, dark fur kept out the Ice Age cold.

FROZEN RHINOS

We know about woolly rhinoceroses from their bodies, which were preserved in frozen soil in Siberia. This means we have a good idea of what these animals looked like: they had two big horns, humped shoulders, and thick legs. Even the horns, made from a hoof-like substance called keratin (like rhinos' horns today), have been preserved in the icy conditions of the frozen north. The horns show signs of wear on one side, so maybe the

WOOLLY RHINOCEROS ▲

rhinos used them to clear snow from the grass as they ate. When people first found ice-preserved rhino horns in the 19th century, they thought they were the claws of giant birds, until whole rhinos were discovered.

Maps throughout indicate contemporary continents where fossils have been found.

LIVED: 350,000 to 10,000 years ago

SIZE: up to 6 feet at the shoulder

WEIGHT: 2 to 3 tons

CREATURE FEATURE: 2 huge horns, the larger one up to 3 feet long

Rhino Horn Spear

In 2014 a 13,300-year-old spear made from a single rhino horn was found in northern Russia. It was almost three feet long. The people who made it might have used it to hunt woolly mammoths.

Sumatran Rhinoceros

Today there are five different kinds of rhinoceros: the black rhino and white rhino (which live in Africa), the Indian and Javan rhinos, and the Sumatran rhino, which is the animal most closely related to the woolly rhino. Sumatran rhinos are the smallest rhino alive today (slightly smaller than a woolly rhinoceros), and have a sparse coat of reddish-colored hair. The Sumatran rhino is critically endangered today; there are fewer than 100 of them left.

Sumatran Rhino ▼

6 ft

GIGANTOPITHECUS

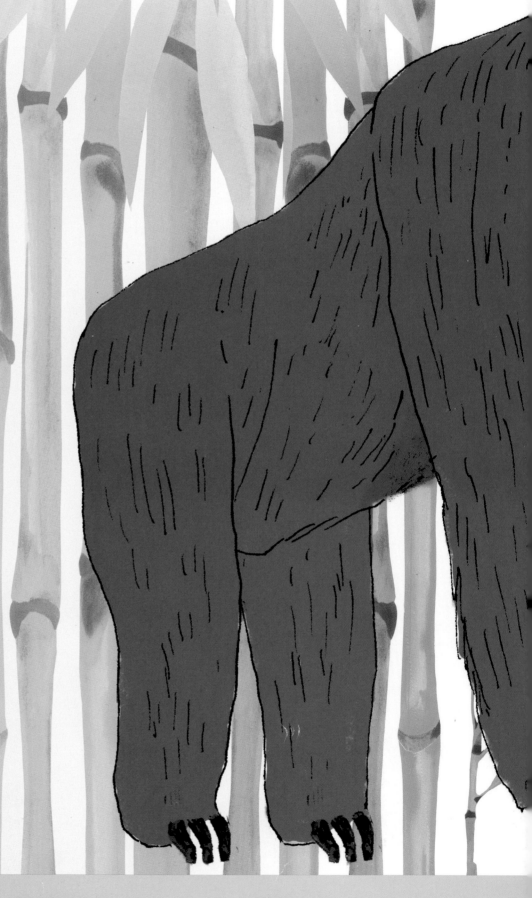

This gigantic ape was, as far as we know, the largest ape that ever lived—a real-life Bigfoot, and the scariest of our closer relatives.

PLANET OF THE APES

When the monkey and ape family first evolved around 60 million years ago, they were small insect- and fruit-eating animals that lived in trees. Some of them stayed that way, while others became much, much bigger. *Gigantopithecus* is the largest ape that's ever been found; its fossils have been discovered in India and Southeast Asia. Although the animals had big teeth and were up to ten feet tall, they were vegetarian and might have been gentle giants like gorillas. (Though gorillas aren't gentle all the time—occasionally they fight to the death.) *Gigantopithecus* probably walked on all fours, like gorillas do today.

LIVED: 9 million to 100,000 years ago
SIZE: up to 10 ft tall

WEIGHT: up to 1,100 lbs
CREATURE FEATURE: giant body and big teeth

BIGFOOT

It's been suggested that *Gigantopithecus* is still alive and responsible for modern sightings of huge, hairy, ape-like creatures known as Bigfoot, Sasquatch, or the Abominable Snowman. This is extremely unlikely!

GIGANTOPITHECUS

ORANGUTAN

Orangutans, the orange-haired apes that live in Borneo and Sumatra, are the closest living relatives of *Gigantopithecus*. Together with gorillas, chimpanzees, and human beings, they are the last surviving great apes. Orangutans are endangered: they are losing their homes as tropical rainforests are being cut down.

ORANGUTAN ▼

10 ft

LIVED: 1.9 million to 10,000 years ago

SIZE: almost 20 feet long

WEIGHT: up to 4.5 tons

CREATURE FEATURE: giant-size armor plating, and claws over 2 ft long

MEGATHERIUM

Thousands of years ago, the gigantic *Megatherium* roamed South America. It looked very much like modern tree sloths do today—except it was nearly the size of an elephant, and far too big and heavy to live in trees. When standing upright on its hind legs it would have been taller than a giraffe.

LAST OF THE GROUND SLOTHS

There were different types of giant ground sloth, and *Megatherium* was the biggest and the last of them—it lived at the same time as humans like us.

◀ *MEGATHERIUM*

ARMORED DEFENSE

Megatherium was vegetarian and used its long arms to pull leaves from the branches of trees. Its shaggy coat concealed an unusual defense: small bony plates underneath its skin that fitted together like armor plating. *Megatherium* also had curved sharp claws that it could use to protect itself from predators.

SMALL SLOTHS

Relatives of these giant sloths are alive today, but the biggest are only about two feet long and 18 pounds in weight. They spend almost all their time hanging from tree branches and barely move. They move so little that moss grows on their fur, making them appear green! Tree sloths climb down to the ground to poop about once a week.

TREE SLOTH ▼

20 ft

GIANT PACARANA

GIANT PACARANA ▶

You might have met some modern-day rodents: pet hamsters, gerbils, or guinea pigs, wild field mice, or muskrats. But hopefully you've never met one that's the size of a cow and weighs a ton!

MEGA RAT

Millions of years ago, mega rodents were living in South America, nibbling things with their enormous teeth. Known as giant pacaranas, they are the largest rodent that's ever lived—at least, as far as we know. A giant pacarana's skull that measures 21 inches long was found—five house mice could line up alongside it. And that's just its head!

LIVED: 4 to 2 million years ago

SIZE: around 10 ft long and 5 ft tall

WEIGHT: 1 ton—we don't know for sure because a complete skeleton has never been found, but this is the average estimate

CREATURE FEATURE: enormous front teeth, measuring 12 in long

Mega Teeth

Giant pacaranas' front teeth measured as long as a ruler. They might have used their ginormous gnashers to fight one another or to defend themselves from predators. They could have also used them to gnaw on wood to build nests, like modern beavers do.

Capybara Cousins

Modern-day capybaras look rather like giant pacaranas. And like giant pacaranas, capybaras live in South America and eat plants. Capybaras are the world's biggest rodents today—they measure up to two feet tall and four feet long, and weigh up to 150 pounds.

◀ Capybara

Giant pacaranas probably spent some of their time in rivers or lakes. Their eyes and nostrils were close to the tops of their heads, so they would have been able to wade into deep water and still breathe and see.

5 ft

ARSINOITHERIUM

More than 30 million years ago, strange plant-eating animals lumbered across northern Africa, armed with some of the most impressive horns ever. They looked like rhinos and lived like hippos, but *Arsinoitherium* was in a class all its own.

WATERY HOME

Arsinoitherium fossils have been found in northern Africa, but when these horned animals lived there the area was covered in mangrove swamps and slow-moving streams for an *Arsinoitherium* to wade through and wallow in. The animals' large feet were built to give good support in wet conditions, and its legs were ideal for swimming but would probably have lumbered along awkwardly on land. So it's likely that *Arsinoitherium*

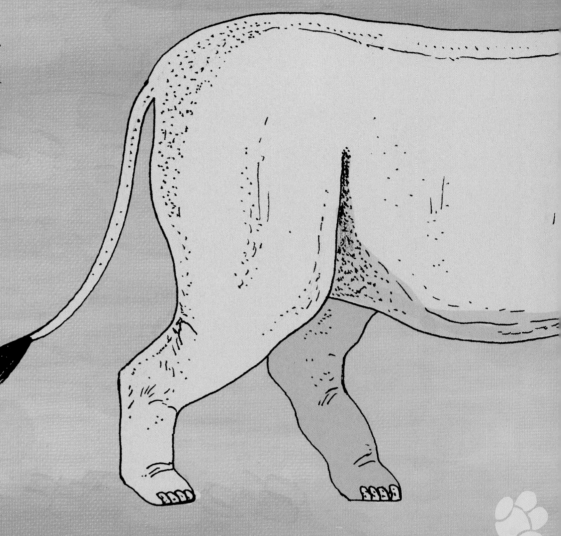

ARSINOITHERIUM ▲

spent most of its time in water, like a hippo. The animal is actually more closely related to elephants than to hippos or rhinos—though the group of mammals to which it belonged has died out completely.

TWIN HORN

The thing you can't help noticing about *Arsinoitherium* is the absolutely massive twin horns on the end of its nose. Unlike rhinoceros horns, which are made of keratin, *Arsinoitherium*'s horns

LIVED: 36 to 30 million years ago
SIZE: over 5 ft tall at the shoulder

WEIGHT: 2.5 tons
CREATURE FEATURE: an enormous double horn

HONKING HORNS

The *Arsinoitherium*'s bony horns were hollow, so the animals might have used them to make a loud, booming call.

HAPPY HIPPOS

Although hippos aren't related to *Arsinoitherium*, they spend most of their time in water, like *Arsinoitherium* did. A hippo can close its nostrils when it is underwater: a useful trick when swimming! Hippos are vegetarian but can be extremely dangerous—they have a 1.6-foot-long, tusk-like tooth that can kill.

HIPPO ▶

were made of bone. The twin horns were so big it must have made it difficult to see straight ahead. Behind them were a pair of much smaller bony horns.

5.5 ft

Lystrosaurus

This ugly-looking reptile is one of the world's greatest survivors. It lived through a mass extinction to become the most common big animal in the Triassic world, wandering the earth in large herds when the first dinosaurs appeared.

Toothless

Lystrosaurus probably had a hard beak (like a turtle's) for eating plants—since it had no teeth, only tusks!

Worldwide Success

Fossils of *Lystrosaurus* have been found in many parts of the world. It was about the size of a large dog, and it's thought to have been the most common land animal on Earth—probably for millions of years!

Lystrosaurus ▲

Lystrosaurus fossils have been found in many parts of the world. ▼

LIVED: 270 to 250 million years ago

SIZE: typically about 3 ft long (ranging from 2 ft to 8 ft)

WEIGHT: up to 200 lbs

CREATURE FEATURE: burrowing legs and claws, stumpy tusks

PUG UGLY

Lystrosaurus was very ugly indeed. It had a long face and tusks that stuck out from its jaw. It looked like a cross between an especially unattractive lizard and a pig.

MASS EXTINCTION

Around 252 million years ago, there was a mass extinction that wiped out more than 90 percent of all the living things on Earth. Somehow, *Lystrosaurus* managed to survive. Its underground lifestyle might have helped: *Lystrosaurus* used its strong front legs to dig burrows, and may have used its tusks to dig up roots. Also, its predators may have died out.

SPINY-TAILED LIZARDS

Like *Lystrosaurus*, spiny-tailed lizards dig burrows. They scramble into their underground homes when danger threatens during the day. Spiny-tailed lizards sometimes hide from predators in rock crevices, and they can puff up their bodies to wedge themselves in! They live in dry parts of Africa and Asia.

SPINY-TAILED LIZARD ▾

3 ft

UINTATHERIUM

These huge, plant-eating, rhino-like animals are some of the strangest looking creatures that ever lived.

LUMPS AND BUMPS

The male *Uintatherium* had one of the oddest heads ever. It was covered in horns and bumps, with three pairs of horns, and huge, tusk-like canine teeth (like a saber-toothed cat's) sticking out of its upper jaw. These strange-looking bits and pieces might seem ugly to us, but to other *Uintatheria* they were absolutely gorgeous: they were probably used for mating

UINTATHERIUM ▶

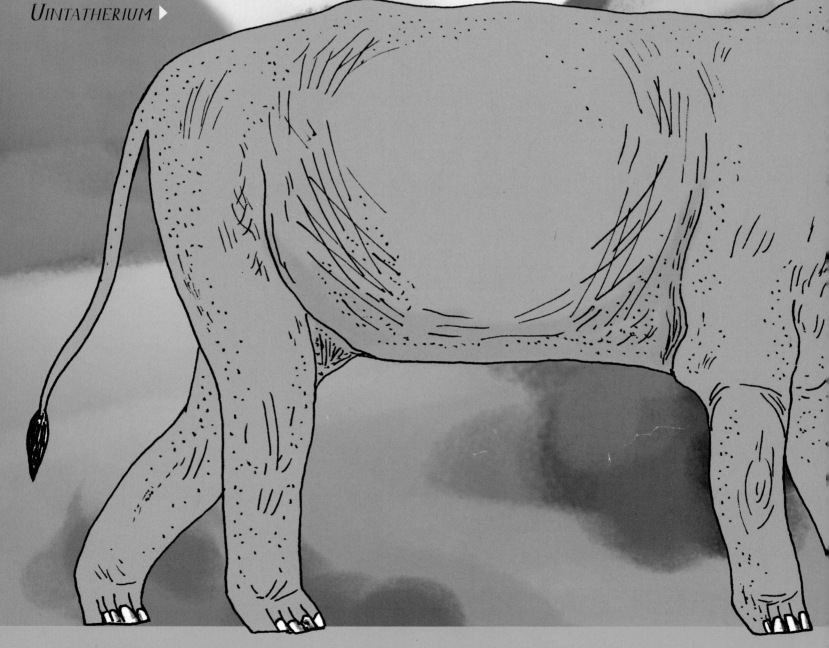

LIVED: 50 to 37 million years ago
SIZE: 13 ft long, 5.6 ft at the shoulder

WEIGHT: up to 2 tons
CREATURE FEATURE: long canine teeth, horns, and bumps

Brain Box

displays, so the more lumpy and bumpy, the better! The horns and tusks might also have been used for defending their territory from other animals.

Whatever their horns were used for, *Uintatheria* probably didn't give it too much thought: they had thick skulls and tiny brains. Their brains were nowhere near as big as the brains of today's grazing animals.

White Rhino

When it was first discovered, scientists thought *Uintatherium* was closely related to modern elephants. It isn't, and scientists argue over where it fits into the mammal family. It looks most like a modern rhinoceros (though it isn't closely related to them either), and it was about the size of a modern white rhino. Sadly, white rhinos are critically endangered because they are hunted for their valuable horns, which are used as medicine or dagger handles in some countries.

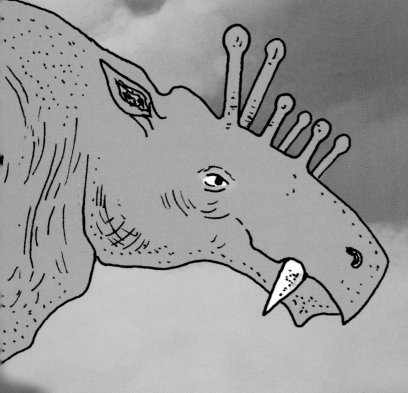

WHITE RHINO ▶

13 ft

THERIZINOSAURUS

Stalking the Mongolian plains 75 million years ago was a dinosaur with sword-like claws nearly three feet long.

CURVED CLAWS

Therizinosaurus's incredibly long claws were curved like vicious swords. When they were first discovered, they were thought to belong to a turtle! They're a puzzle to scientists because they weren't capable of tearing flesh—in fact, *Therizinosaurus* wasn't even a meat-eater. The claws might have been for display, or to intimidate predators, or maybe the dinosaur used them to pull down leaves from trees to eat. *Therizinosaurus*'s plant-based diet is also a mystery because other dinosaurs in the same family group are predators.

THERIZINOSAURUS ▶

LIVED: 85 to 70 million years ago

SIZE: 33 ft long

WEIGHT: up to 5 tons

CREATURE FEATURE: curved, sharp claws nearly 3 ft long—the longest known claws of any animal

WAS IT A BIRD?

Therizinosaurus was similar to bird-like dinosaurs, so some experts think it might have had feathers.

CASSOWARY

Cassowaries have some of the longest claws in the animal kingdom today, though nowhere near as long as *Therizinosaurus*'s. A cassowary is a flightless bird over six feet tall that lives in Australia and New Guinea. The birds are shy, but the middle claws on their feet are four inches long and could be deadly to a human.

CASSOWARY ▶

33 ft

Epigaulus

You'd be surprised to see a hamster with horns, but, believe it or not, horned rodents did once exist! These small mammals were busy digging down into deep holes in North America millions of years ago.

Epigaulus ▶

LIVED: 16 to 5 million years ago
SIZE: 1 ft

WEIGHT: over 6 lbs
CREATURE FEATURE:
the only rodents with horns!

BUILDING BURROWS

Epigaulus was built for burrowing. It had broad paws used for shovelling, and long claws for digging down into the earth. Its big gnawing front teeth—like a rat's or a rabbit's—might have been used for digging too, perhaps chomping through any tree roots that got in the way.

HORNED RODENT

Epigaulus's horns could have helped with digging, but their position facing backwards on the front of the animal's head makes this unlikely. They were probably used for defense, as other horned mammals use them today. As well as being the only horned rodent that we know about, *Epigaulus* is also the smallest horned mammal.

GOPHER

In North America, where *Epigaulus* once dug its underground chambers, burrowing rodents called gophers live today. They live on plants, earthworms, and insects and dig huge networks of underground tunnels, known as gopher towns. People often see them as a pest because they eat farm crops and garden vegetables and can destroy whole fields of crops as they tunnel underneath eating the roots. A gopher stores food in its cheek pouches so that it can take food back to its burrow.

◀ GOPHER

1 ft

Paraceratherium

The largest land mammal that's ever lived stood taller than a house! It made the earth shake as it stomped around the Mongolian grasslands munching plants 30 million years ago.

PARACERATHERIUM ▶

Rhino Relative

Paraceratherium might look like it's related to elephants, but in fact it's a type of hornless rhinoceros.

LIVED: 30 to 25 million years ago

SIZE: 16 ft tall at the shoulder

WEIGHT: 15 tons or maybe more . . .

CREATURE FEATURE: giant-sized—the biggest land mammal ever

Big Beasts

Mammals started off small—they first appeared during the time of the dinosaurs as little ratlike creatures. But they got much, much bigger. *Paraceratherium* was 16 feet tall: the biggest a land mammal has ever grown to be. A *Paraceratherium*'s head was the same length as an average ten-year-old child! It was vegetarian and probably spent a lot of time eating plants to keep its enormous, bulky body going. *Paraceratherium*'s long neck meant it could reach high up—26 feet or more—for leaves that no other animal could reach. It could reach even higher than a giraffe can today!

African Elephants

Today's largest land animals are African elephants. These huge beasts are strong enough to push over and pick up trees. They're still not as big as *Paraceratherium*, though—they measure a maximum of 13 feet tall, and just over seven tons in weight. The trunk of an African elephant contains about 100,000 different muscles! It is used for smelling, breathing, trumpeting, drinking, grabbing food, and playing.

▼ African elephant

16 ft

21

DOEDICURUS

Doedicurus was an armadillo the size of a family car! It trundled about the grasslands of South America, feasting on plants, safe from predators inside its heavy-duty armor plating.

SUIT OF ARMOR

This giant armadillo had a shell made from bony plates an inch thick or more, like the armor-plated suit of a medieval knight. Underneath this protective armor, *Doedicurus* had a thick layer of fat, which acted as a shock absorber against impact. The armor was good for keeping predators at bay, but made the animal very heavy and slow-moving.

 ▲ *DOEDICURUS*

LIVED: 2 million to 11,000 years ago
SIZE: 13 ft

WEIGHT: 4,000 to 5,000 lbs
CREATURE FEATURE: armor plating and a fearsome tail

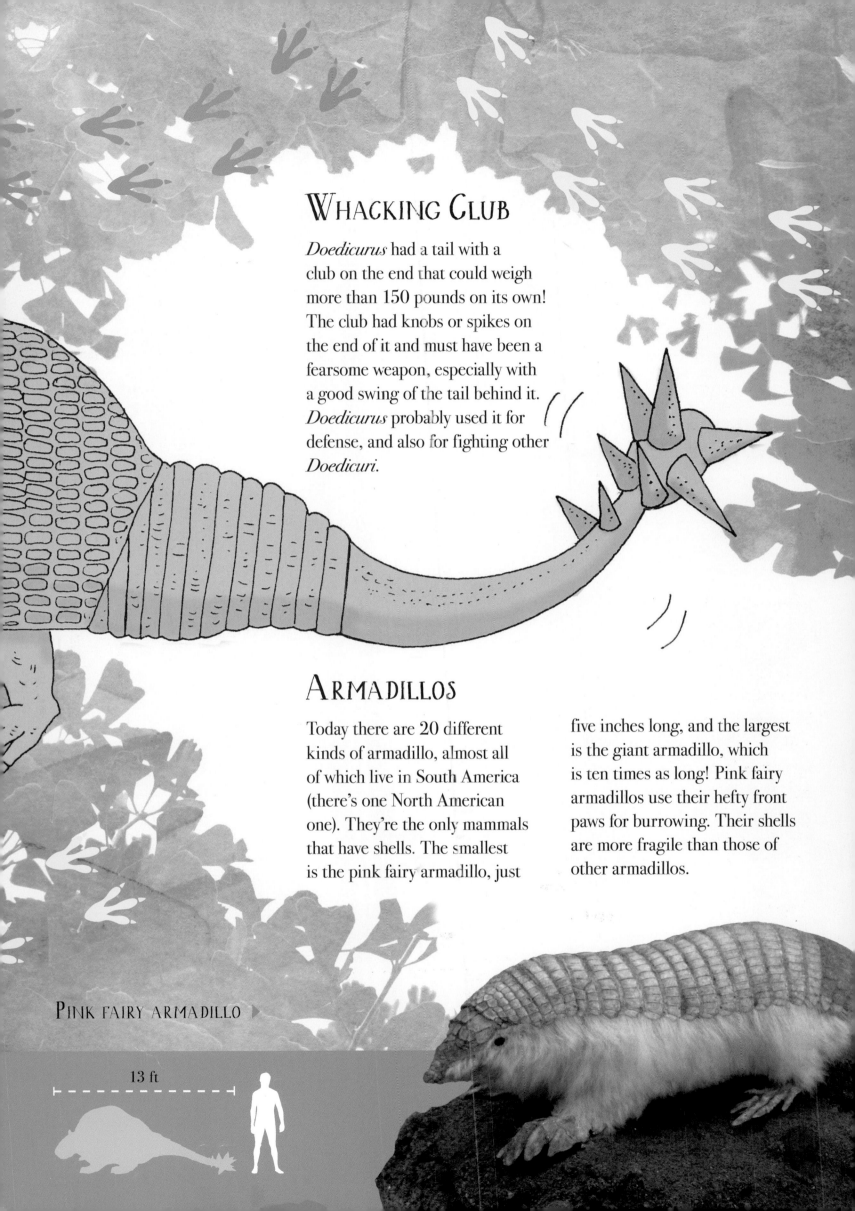

WHACKING CLUB

Doedicurus had a tail with a club on the end that could weigh more than 150 pounds on its own! The club had knobs or spikes on the end of it and must have been a fearsome weapon, especially with a good swing of the tail behind it. *Doedicurus* probably used it for defense, and also for fighting other *Doedicuri*.

ARMADILLOS

Today there are 20 different kinds of armadillo, almost all of which live in South America (there's one North American one). They're the only mammals that have shells. The smallest is the pink fairy armadillo, just five inches long, and the largest is the giant armadillo, which is ten times as long! Pink fairy armadillos use their hefty front paws for burrowing. Their shells are more fragile than those of other armadillos.

PINK FAIRY ARMADILLO ▶

13 ft

IRISH ELK

◀ IRISH ELK

LIVED: 500,000 to 7,000 years ago

SIZE: up to 7 ft at the shoulder

WEIGHT: up to 1500 lbs

CREATURE FEATURE: enormous antlers 12 ft across

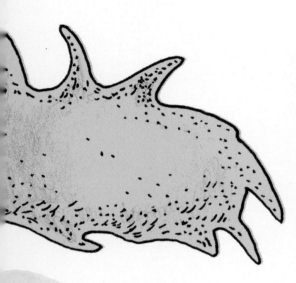

MISTAKEN IDENTITY

Irish elk weren't really elk, but deer, and, though they did live in Ireland, they were also found in many other parts of Europe and as far away as Russia and northern Africa. They got their common name, Irish elk, because so many fossils have been found preserved in peat bogs in Ireland.

MEGA MOOSE

Moose are the largest member of the deer family alive today. They are almost as tall as their extinct Irish elk relatives, at up to six and a half feet at the shoulder. Their antlers are impressive, but still only half the size of the Irish elk's! Moose are surprisingly good swimmers—they can swim for several miles and even submerge themselves completely under water for half a minute or more at a time.

These huge animals were among the largest deer that ever lived. Humans lived at the same time as Irish elks and hunted them for food.

IMPRESSIVE ANTLERS

The Irish elk's antlers probably grew to be so enormous (more than 12 feet wide), because they were important in mating displays: the bigger the male deer's antlers, the more popular they were with the females. The deer with the biggest antlers were fathers of the most baby deer, and so passed on their huge antler genes.

MOOSE ▶

7 ft

CHALICOTHERIUM

This unusual creature was an enormous vegetarian mammal that lurched along munching leaves.

HORSE SLOTH

Standing on its hind legs, *Chalicotherium* was taller than an average ceiling and had a long face a bit like a horse's—in fact, the two animals are related. But the strangest thing about this animal was that its clawed front limbs were much longer than its back ones. When it walked on all fours, it walked on its knuckles, with its hands twisted inwards. It looked a bit like a cross between a horse and a sloth.

JUICY PLANTS

An adult *Chalicotherium* didn't have any front teeth at all, and fossilized back teeth don't show much sign of wear. So it's likely that the animal sat on its hind legs to feed and used its long clawed arms to reach the highest branches, out of reach of other plant eaters, where the tastiest and most tender leaves could be found. With such a large body to keep going, *Chalicotherium* probably spent all its waking life either eating or looking for food.

CHALICOTHERIUM ▶

LIVED: 28 to 5 million years ago
SIZE: 6.5 ft tall

WEIGHT: 1760 lbs
CREATURE FEATURE: long clawed arms

▲ ANTEATER

GIANT ANTEATERS

Chalicotherium is related to horses, not anteaters. But giant anteaters have something in common with *Chalicotherium*— they walk on their knuckles too. These anteaters also have long claws, which they tuck under their hands when they're walking. Anteaters have no teeth, so they use their long tongues to lap up roughly 35,000 ants (or termites) each day. An anteater can spend only one minute eating from an anthill—otherwise the ant stings become too painful.

FRONT TEETH

A young *Chalicotherium* did have front teeth. By the time it was grown up, it was tall enough to grab the tenderest leaves and didn't need cutting teeth anymore.

6.5 ft

WOOLLY MAMMOTH

WOOLLY MAMMOTH ▶

LIVED: 120,000 to 10,000 years ago, though one small group lived on Wrangel Island in the Arctic until around 2000 BC!

SIZE: up to 11 ft at the shoulder

WEIGHT: 6.6 tons

CREATURE FEATURE: thick, shaggy fur and huge tusks

These giant, shaggy tuskers stomped around Europe, Asia, and North America at the same time as our own prehistoric relatives.

Cold Bottom

Woolly mammoths were well adapted to the icy conditions. They even had a special flap under their tails that protected their bottoms from the cold!

Ice Age

Woolly mammoths were about the same size as modern African elephants, but they had to contend with very cold temperatures, which isn't easy when you're enormous. Their thick, dense fur had an outer layer 12 inches long, covering a chubby layer of body fat to keep them warm. Their ears were much smaller than Indian elephants' ears today. Smaller ears are less prone to frostbite and reduce heat loss. The animals' huge tusks might have been used to clear snow, and also to dig for plants underneath frozen ground. It was a hard life in the cold, and woolly mammoths had to eat what they could find: special grinding teeth allowed them to eat even the toughest plants.

Mammoth Hunt

People hunted mammoths for food, used their furry coats to keep warm, and built huts out of mammoth bones. Mammoths were so important to people that our ancestors painted them on cave walls thousands of years ago.

Asian Relatives

Woolly mammoths are more closely related to Asian elephants than African ones. Asian elephants are slightly smaller than their African cousins, and unlike them, they have been trained to move heavy objects, carry people on their backs, and even charge into battle!

▼ ASIAN ELEPHANT

11 ft

GIANT KANGAROO

The kangaroo family includes cute, furry little dwarf wallabies the size of a rabbit, and hulking great red kangaroos the size of a person. But this kangaroo would hop over the lot—if it could actually hop. Scientists aren't sure how it got around.

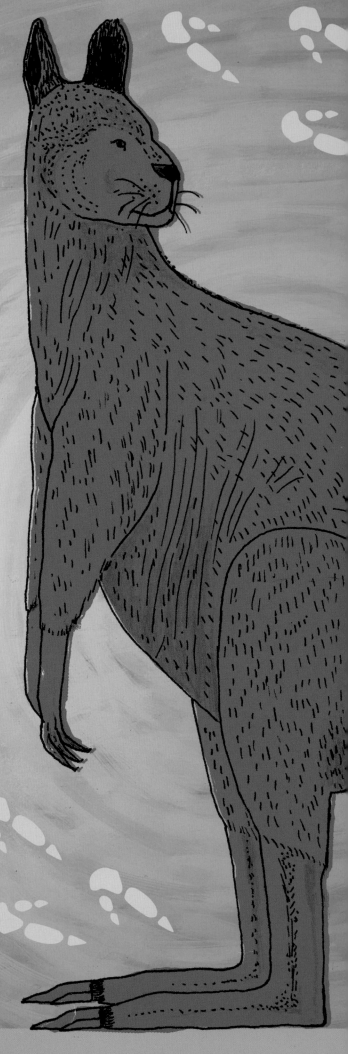

GIANT KANGAROO

LIVED: 300,000 to 500,000 years ago

SIZE: up to 10 ft tall

WEIGHT: up to 530 lbs

CREATURE FEATURE: huge hind legs, long fingers for grabbing food

GREAT JUMPERS

Red kangaroos today can jump as high as a person and cover 25 feet in a single leap. They can bound along at speeds of over 35 miles an hour. The bulk of the giant kangaroo probably meant that it couldn't move that fast and maybe couldn't hop at all.

WHOPPING HOPPER

This whopper of a kangaroo was several feet taller than a modern red kangaroo, with giant hind legs to match. The thick bones of its fossilized skeleton suggest that its body was also a lot bulkier. Modern kangaroos have fairly small, stiff arms, but the giant kangaroo had long arms with grasping hands and two especially long fingers—it probably used them to pull down tall branches to get at the tasty leaves.

RED KANGAROO

This is the largest animal in the kangaroo family alive today and can grow to over five feet tall. Although they're plant eaters, male red kangaroos can be aggressive: they fight by kicking out with their legs and can bite and scratch with their huge claws. Female kangaroos can delay a joey developing if their environment is especially hard to survive in (for example, if there's a sudden shortage in water).

RED KANGAROO

10 ft

DREADNOUGHTUS

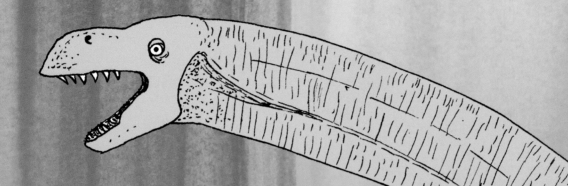

These absolutely massive dinosaurs must have been an impressive sight as they lumbered through South America 77 million years ago. *Dreadnoughtus* is the largest dinosaur so far discovered and makes the largest land mammal (see page 26) look like a tiny baby.

GINORMOUS DINOSAUR

Other giant dinosaurs have been found, but we can only learn about them from a few remaining fossilized bones. Imagine the dinosaur hunters' delight when they discovered two almost complete fossil skeletons in Argentina in 2005—fossils of the biggest dinosaur so far discovered. *Dreadnoughtus* is part of the same group of dinosaurs (sauropods) that includes *Diplodocus*, but is twice as heavy. Scientists can tell from the fossilized bones that these specimens hadn't yet stopped growing—so an adult *Dreadnoughtus* would have been even bigger!

DREADNOUGHTUS ▶

FEARLESS

"Dreadnought," a name given to gigantic battleships in the early 20th century, means "fear nothing." It's unlikely that *Dreadnoughtus* had much to be scared of!

LIVED: 84 to 66 million years ago
SIZE: 85 ft long

WEIGHT: 30 to 40 tons
CREATURE FEATURE: absolutely huge!

BLUE WHALE

The biggest animal around today—in fact, the biggest animal that's ever lived—is the blue whale. Its heart is as big as a car, its tongue weighs as much as a rhino, and even a newborn baby blue whale is 25 feet long! These big beauties measure up to 100 feet long and weigh up to 200 tons—that's over three times a *Dreadnoughtus*!

BLUE WHALE

85 ft

PREHISTORIC SEA CREATURES

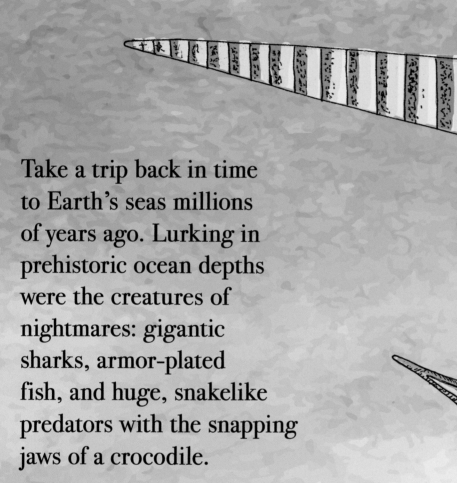

Take a trip back in time to Earth's seas millions of years ago. Lurking in prehistoric ocean depths were the creatures of nightmares: gigantic sharks, armor-plated fish, and huge, snakelike predators with the snapping jaws of a crocodile.

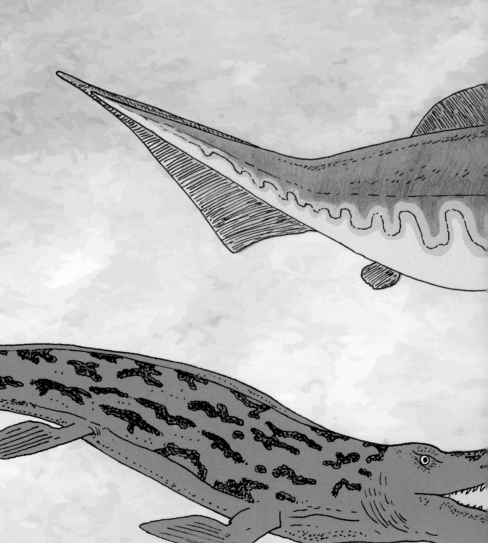

MEGALODON

A few million years ago, an enormous flesh-eating shark hunted the seas—one of the most terrifying predators that's ever lived. It made today's great white sharks look like goldfish.

GIANT JAWS

Like all sharks' skeletons, *Megalodon* skeletons are made from cartilage, which is much more difficult than bone to turn into a fossil. So we mostly know about *Megalodons* from their teeth, which are sharp, saw-edged, and absolutely huge. The longest one ever found is more than six inches long, and *Megalodon* had around 276 of them! It's thought that a *Megalodon* measured longer than a bus, and the biggest had jaws that were over six feet wide. They were so big and scary that they ate large whales for breakfast! Whale bone fossils have been found with bite marks that match *Megalodon*'s teeth.

MEGALODON ▲

Megalodon fossils have been found worldwide! ▼

LIVED: 23 to 2.6 million years ago
SIZE: between 40 and 70 ft long

WEIGHT: possibly between 50 and 115 tons
CREATURE FEATURE: huge jaws and mega teeth

GREAT WHITE

Megalodon is the largest shark ever. Today's biggest shark, the great white, is puny by comparison—great whites grow to about 15 feet long, which is less than half the length of a *Megalodon*! A great white has roughly 300 teeth arranged in several rows.

▲ GREAT WHITE

TEETH OR TONGUE?

Megalodon hunted in seas all over the world, and people have been finding *Megalodon* teeth for centuries. Before the 17th century, people thought they were the petrified tongues of dragons.

50 ft

CAMEROCERAS

Around 450 million years ago, *Cameroceras* was the biggest—and meanest—animal alive. It was a massive shellfish, possibly up to 20 feet long, and a fearsome predator.

BEAKS AND TENTACLES

Cameroceras's hard shell protected its soft body. It had grasping tentacles to grab its fishy prey, like today's squid. The tentacles were up to three feet long and had grooved surfaces, rather than the suckers that squid and octopus tentacles have now.

Cameroceras would grab a fish or a trilobite, then cram it into its sharp beak and devour it. To chase after its prey, *Cameroceras* had an unusual method of swimming: it was jet propelled, forcing water backwards through a tube to push itself forwards.

UNICORN HORNS

Fossils of their long, pointed shells were mistaken for unicorn horns! It's thought that the biggest *Cameroceras* specimens didn't move about much—they lurked near the sea floor waiting to ambush passing prey.

LIVED: 470 to 425 million years ago

SIZE: up to 20 feet long—estimates are made from shell fragments

WEIGHT: estimated at up to 300 lbs

CREATURE FEATURE: 3-foot-long grasping tentacles and jet propulsion

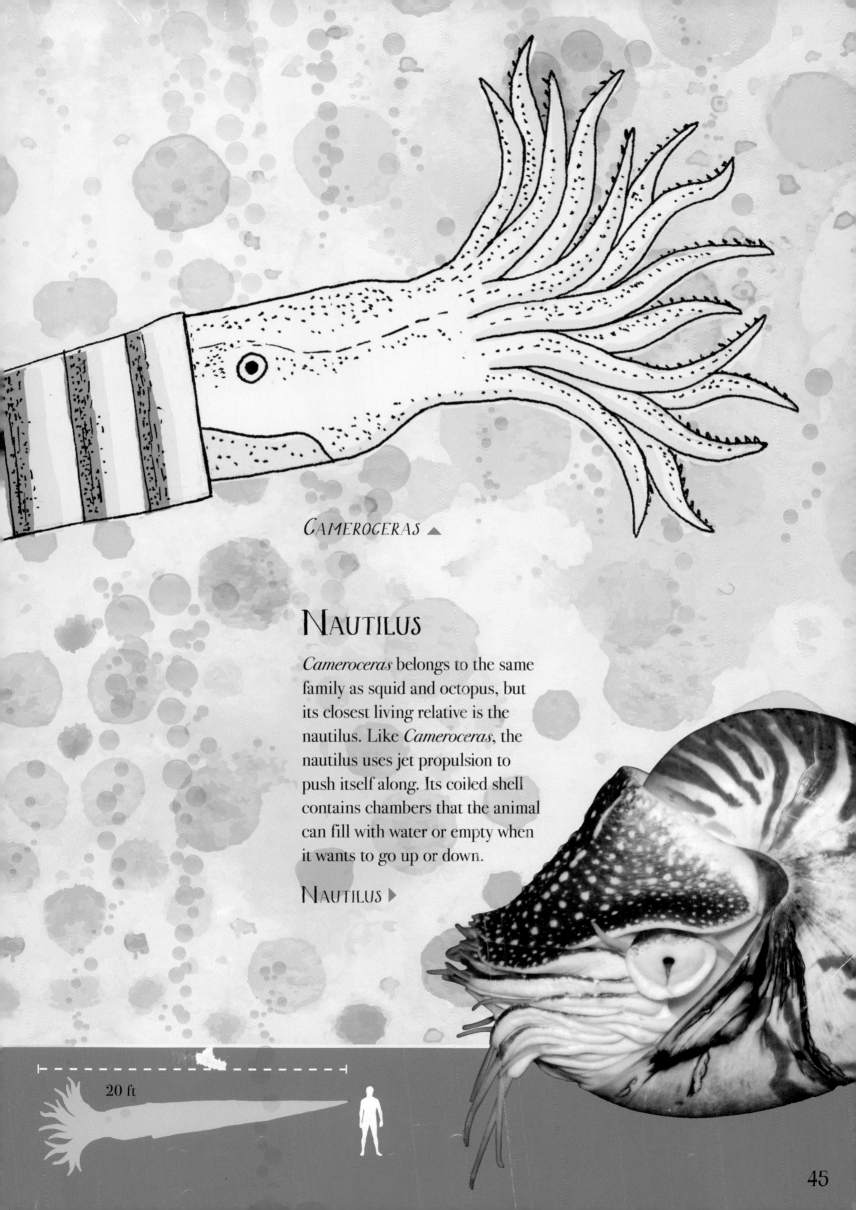

CAMEROCERAS ▲

NAUTILUS

Cameroceras belongs to the same family as squid and octopus, but its closest living relative is the nautilus. Like *Cameroceras*, the nautilus uses jet propulsion to push itself along. Its coiled shell contains chambers that the animal can fill with water or empty when it wants to go up or down.

NAUTILUS ▶

20 ft

DUNKLEOSTEUS

This absolutely enormous armored fish patrolled the seas like a super-scary, fish-chomping submarine. It was the biggest marine predator of its time.

SICK BALLS

Because *Dunkleosteus* swallowed huge chunks of meat without chewing, it was often sick. Lots of fossilized *Dunkleosteus* sick balls have been discovered, which have revealed that the armored fish ate almost anything, including sharks and even its own kind.

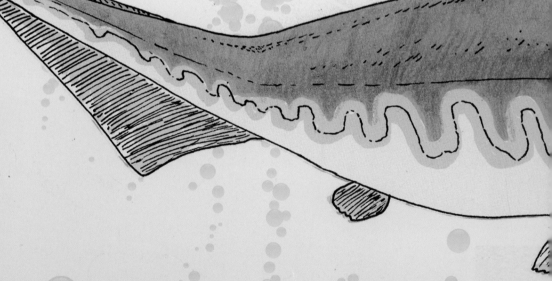

SLICING BONES

Dunkleosteus was the biggest of a group of armor-plated fish: it had a protective armor made of bony plates that covered its head and the front of its body, though it was so big that it couldn't have had much need to protect itself. Instead of teeth, it had sharp plates made of bone which it used to bite through its prey. The lack of teeth meant that *Dunkleosteus* couldn't chew: it sliced up food and then swallowed it in chunks.

DUNKLEOSTEUS

LIVED: 370 to 360 million years ago
SIZE: up to 33 ft long

WEIGHT: up to 4 tons
CREATURE FEATURE: armor plating and slicing jaws

BULL SHARK

SHARK COMPETITION

Some of *Dunkleosteus*'s victims were early sharks. But in the end the bony fish died out, most probably due to competition from sharks, which were faster and better hunters. Today there are more than 400 shark species, but not all of them are predators. The bull shark is one of the most aggressive sharks in the world, and one of the three that are most dangerous to humans. Bull sharks get their name from their blunt snout and because they often head butt their prey!

33 ft

ARCHELON

Around 70 million years ago, a gigantic turtle the size of a small car cruised North America's shallow seas.

PREDATOR AND PREY

Archelon was a meat eater. Its powerful, razor-sharp beak was strong enough to slice shell and bone, and it probably fed on shellfish, such as ammonites, fish, and jellyfish. But there were bigger predators than *Archelon* around: huge, flesh-eating sea lizards were waiting to snap it up! *Archelon*'s rubbery shell didn't protect it as well as a hard one, and it couldn't withdraw its flippers and head inside it. Lots of *Archelon* fossils have been found, and many are missing one or more flippers, probably due to predators like *Tylosaurus* (see page 50).

ARCHELON ▲

LIVED: 75 to 65 million years ago

SIZE: 12 to 15 ft long

WEIGHT: 4,500 lbs

CREATURE FEATURE: huge leathery shells and four massive flippers

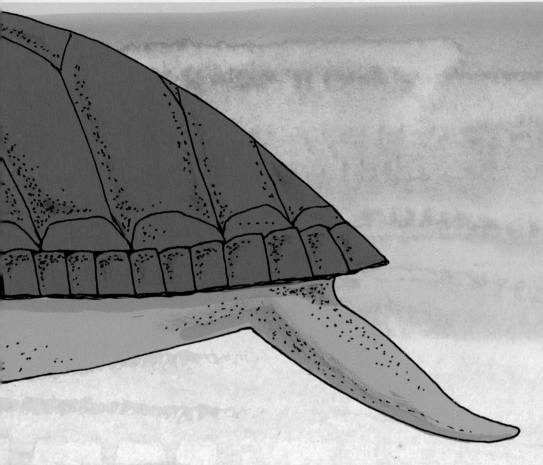

LEATHERBACK TURTLE

Leatherback turtles have been around for more than 100 million years. Their shells, which can measure up to seven feet long, are flexible and leathery, like *Archelon*'s shell. Leatherback turtles can stay underwater for up to 85 minutes, and can dive as deep as 4,000 feet! Their favorite food is jellyfish—sadly, turtles sometimes eat floating plastic carrier bags, mistaking them for jellyfish, and die. Leatherback turtles are now endangered animals.

LEATHERBACK TURTLE ▼

OLD TURTLE

Like turtles today, *Archelon* laid its eggs on sandy beaches. When they hatched, the baby turtles had to avoid predators on the beach and in the sea. But if they did survive to adulthood, *Archelon* could have a long life: some lived to be 100 years old.

15 ft

TYLOSAURUS

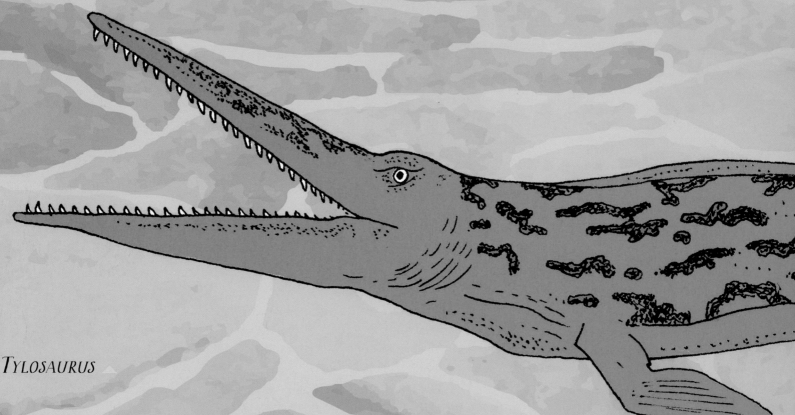

TYLOSAURUS

This sea predator was like an especially huge and vicious sea snake, but with the massive head and long, snapping jaws of a crocodile. It hunted the seas in the time of the dinosaurs.

OCEAN PREDATORS

Tylosaurus had a long body, a bit like a modern sea snake's, but much, much longer and bulkier. It powered through the Cretaceous seas with four streamlined flippers and a huge, rudder-like tail. To help it find its prey, *Tylosaurus* had large eyes and excellent vision. It preyed on fish, birds, and turtles as well as bigger animals—sharks as long as 20 feet, and large birds and pterosaurs that swooped too close in search of fish.

LIVED: 89 to 65 million years ago

SIZE: up to about 45 ft long

WEIGHT: roughly 7 tons (but estimates vary)

CREATURE FEATURE: crocodile-like head, extra teeth, flippers, massive snake-like body . . . this predator had everything!

Great Gnashers

As well as the terrifying array of cone-shaped teeth in its jaws, *Tylosaurus* also had two rows of teeth on the roof of its mouth, so that once it had its prey in its jaws there was absolutely no escape!

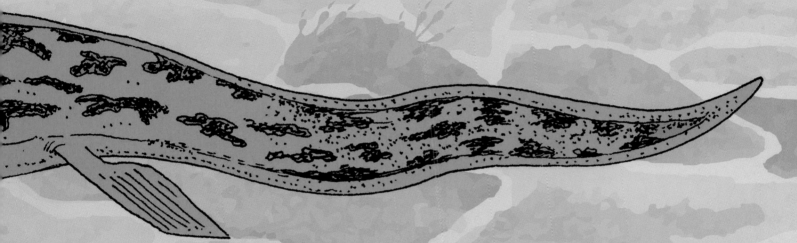

Gila Monsters

Tylosaurus wasn't a dinosaur (dinosaurs are land animals), but a mosasaur, which are related to modern day Gila monsters. These lizards, which grow to around 22 inches long, are some of the world's few venomous lizards. Instead of injecting venom through fangs, Gila monsters bite then hang on and chew, injecting venom into the wound through grooves in their teeth!

GILA MONSTER ▲

45 ft

51

LEEDSICHTHYS

This giant of the deep cruised the world's oceans in the time of the dinosaurs. It was one of the biggest fish ever.

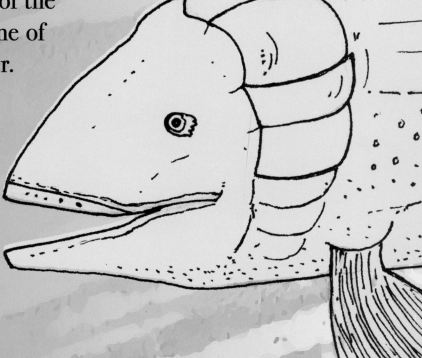

LEEDSICHTHYS ▶

SIZE MATTERS

Leedsichthys was huge. Just how huge is difficult to say, because some of its skeleton was made of cartilage (like shark skeletons), which doesn't fossilize well. At one time, the ginormous fish was thought to be almost 90 feet long—about the size of a blue whale—which would make it the biggest fish of all time. More recently, the *Leedsichthys* has been downsized to around 56 feet long. That's still bigger than the world's biggest fish today, but maybe not as long as the biggest fish we know about, the *Megalodon* (see page 42). So poor old *Leedsichthys* might have to take second prize instead of first . . .

LIVED: 165 to 155 million years ago
SIZE: 26 to 55 ft long

WEIGHT: up to 27 tons
CREATURE FEATURE: the world's biggest sieve!

SIEVING THE SEA

Leedsichthys fed on plankton—microscopic living things floating in the sea. To sieve the seawater for plankton, it used a mesh in the back of its throat made of thousands of fine bony teeth. *Leedsichthys* had around 40,000 of them!

WHALE SHARK

The biggest fish in the sea today is also a plankton feeder—the whale shark. These enormous creatures can be up to 40 feet long and weigh 21 tons. Their mouths measure up to five feet across, so a *Leedsichthys*'s mouth must have been even bigger! Whale sharks can't swallow a human being, even by mistake: their mouths are huge, but their throats are small.

WHALE SHARK ▾
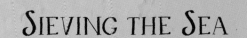

55 ft

ELASMOSAURUS

If you think a giraffe has a long neck, here is a *really* long one! *Elasmosaurus* was an ocean lizard with the longest neck in the animal kingdom.

SURPRISING PREDATOR

Elasmosaurus hunted the seas for fish and other creatures. It might have swum underneath shoals of fish, sneakily floating its head up to grab the unsuspecting fish above it. To help it digest its food and to help weigh it down so it could dive deeper, *Elasmosaurus* swallowed smooth pebbles. One fossil was found with 250 pebbles in its stomach.

HEAD OR TAIL?

Elasmosaurus had more than 70 vertebrae in its neck. People (and giraffes!) have seven. When the first fossilized *Elasmosaurus* was put together, the head was put on the wrong end, because the neck was so long it was thought to be a tail!

LIVED: 85 to 65 million years ago

SIZE: up to 50 ft long

WEIGHT: 2 tons

CREATURE FEATURE: extraordinarily long neck

54

A Lot of Neck

Elasmosaurus belongs to the plesiosaurs, a family group which includes some animals with big heads and short necks, and others—like *Elasmosaurus*—with small heads and long necks. As far as we know, *Elasmosaurus*'s neck was the longest of the long. It could measure up to 25 feet!

ELASMOSAURUS ▲

Giraffes

These African giants can measure up to 18 feet tall, and their necks can reach an incredible six feet. Even a giraffe's legs are taller than most people—six feet long. They also have very long tongues for grasping leaves—up to 21 inches in length! Their tongues are blue in color.

Giraffe ▶

50 ft

PREHISTORIC
PREDATORS

A wide and terrifying variety of predators have stalked the earth in the millions of years since animals first crawled onto land. Slimy, sharp-toothed amphibians lay in wait to snap up prey, massive snakes that could crush a crocodile hunted the jungles, and saber-toothed cats prowled America at the same time as our ancestors.

ANDREWSARCHUS

Think of the scariest land predator you can: maybe a wolf, a tiger, or a polar bear. Now double it in size, add an enormous head full of sharp teeth, and you're somewhere near *Andrewsarchus*, which may have been the biggest meat-eating land mammal of all time.

BIG HEAD

Andrewsarchus had a monster head: its skull measured nearly three feet long and two feet wide. Its massive jaws were full of teeth—long, sharp canine teeth for gripping, and flat back teeth for crushing bone.

ANDREWSARCHUS ▶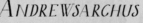

LIVED: 40 to 35 million years ago

SIZE: possibly up to 12 ft long, and maybe up to 6 ft tall at the shoulder

WEIGHT: estimated at 400 to 1000 lbs

CREATURE FEATURE: huge jaws and mega teeth

SURPRISING DESCENDANTS

Although it may have looked like a wolf or a big cat, *Andrewsarchus* is actually the distant ancestor of hoofed mammals such as pigs, deer, cows, and also, believe it or not, whales (whose ancestors lived on land before their legs evolved into flippers). Instead of claws on its toes, *Andrewsarchus* probably had short hooves. It probably couldn't have run very fast, so it might have eaten dead animals more than live ones, and eaten plants and insects as well.

POLAR BEAR

The largest living land predator is the polar bear. These huge creatures weigh up to 1500 lbs, measure up to nine feet long, and stand about the height of an adult human at the shoulder. But *Andrewsarchus* could have eaten one for breakfast!

12 ft

POLAR BEAR ▶

59

SARCOSUCHUS

A hundred million years ago, this gigantic, dinosaur-eating reptile lurked menacingly in rivers and lakes.

KNOBBLY NOSE

Sarcosuchus had a snout as long as a tall person, and on the end of it was a big knobbly growth called a bulla. Modern gharials—a type of crocodile—have the same thing. No one knows exactly what bullas are for, but it might have helped *Sarcosuchus* to sniff out its prey.

GIANT JAWS

Sarcosuchus's skull was about the same length as today's dwarf crocodiles—six feet long! *Sarcosuchus* was very similar to an enormous crocodile, though it wasn't in the same family group as today's crocs and alligators. Like crocodiles, it probably spent a lot of time submerged in water, lying in wait for its prey to get close enough to its massive jaws. On *Sarcosuchus*'s menu were fish, turtles, dinosaurs, and pterosaurs. Fossils have been found in the Sahara Desert and also South America, because when *Sarcosuchus* was alive the two continents were joined together.

LIVED: 121 to 93 million years ago
SIZE: 40 ft long

WEIGHT: 8 to 10 tons
CREATURE FEATURE: long knobbly snout, sharp teeth, and snapping jaws

SALTWATER CROCODILE

Saltwater crocodiles are the biggest crocodiles alive today. They can measure up to 21 feet long and weigh a ton, but they're mere babies in comparison to *Sarcosuchus*. Only one percent of saltwater crocodiles reach adulthood. The hatchlings are often eaten by predators—including other male saltwater crocodiles and even their own fathers!

SALTWATER CROCODILE ▼

40 ft

GIGANOTOSAURUS

It's South America in the time of the dinosaurs. A thunderous roar echoes across the landscape and the ground begins to shake . . . Run for cover, because the biggest land predator of all time is on its way!

FEARSOME PREDATOR

As flesh-eating monsters go, *Giganotosaurus* was definitely one of the best. It had a good sense of smell and sharp eyesight to sniff out and spot its prey and was speedy enough to catch it— some scientists reckon it could run as fast as 31 miles an hour.

GIGANOTOSAURUS GANGS

Giganotosaurus probably travelled in small groups to attack in packs, like especially scary giant reptilian wolves! They would have been able to kill even the biggest plant-eating dinosaurs.

GIGANOTOSAURUS ▲

LIVED: 99 to 97 million years ago
SIZE: 40 to 43 ft long

WEIGHT: up to 14 tons
CREATURE FEATURE: serrated teeth 8 inches long, sharp claws

TERRIFYING T-REX

Before *Giganotosaurus* was discovered in 1993, a different dinosaur was thought to be the largest predatory land animal ever: *Tyrannosaurus rex*. At around 40 feet long and weighing up to nine tons, T-rex wasn't quite as enormous as *Giganotosaurus*. It lived in North America millions of years after *Giganotosaurus* died out, so the two dinosaurs wouldn't have met. T-rex is probably the world's most famous dinosaur, because so many almost complete fossil skeletons have been found.

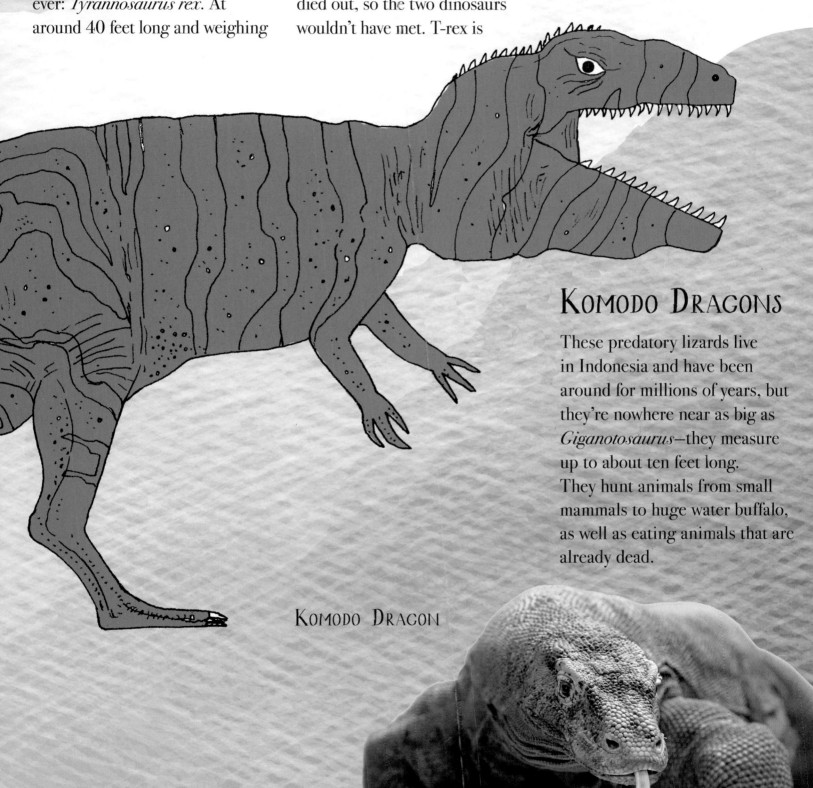

KOMODO DRAGON

KOMODO DRAGONS

These predatory lizards live in Indonesia and have been around for millions of years, but they're nowhere near as big as *Giganotosaurus*—they measure up to about ten feet long. They hunt animals from small mammals to huge water buffalo, as well as eating animals that are already dead.

40 ft

SMILODON

Imagine taking a walk through the fields when suddenly you're faced with a massive big cat with foot-long canine teeth! Our ancestors really did encounter this terrifying predator thousands of years ago.

FEARSOME PREDATORS

Saber-toothed cats died out in Africa and Europe before people evolved, but in the Americas two kinds of *Smilodon* lived at the same time as people. These toothy-grinned big cats probably dropped from trees to ambush deer, horses, and young bison. They may have lived in groups and hunted in packs, as lions do today.

NOT SO TOUGH TEETH

The *Smilodon*'s famous sword-like teeth were so big they reached down below the animal's jaw, but they were quite delicate and couldn't be used to crunch bone. *Smilodons* may have slashed prey with the saber teeth, then let them bleed to death.

LIVED: 2.5 million to 10,000 years ago

SIZE: about 3 ft at the shoulder and almost 6 ft long

WEIGHT: up to 600 lbs

CREATURE FEATURE: enormous canine teeth!

SMILODON

SIBERIAN TIGERS

Although *Smilodon* is often called a saber-toothed tiger, it's only very distantly related to modern big cats. The biggest of the big cats today is the Siberian tiger, which can weigh 660 pounds and measure more than ten feet long (plus its enormous three-foot-long tail)—which makes it a bit bigger than a *Smilodon*.

SIBERIAN TIGER ▶

6 ft

TITANOBOA

Think of a snake . . . then think of a really big snake . . . then multiply it a few times . . . and you're still probably not anywhere near imagining the huge, crocodile-crushing *Titanoboa*.

TITANIC SNAKE

The *Titanoboa* is the largest snake ever discovered. It once slithered through the rainforests of South America, hunting turtles, fish, and even huge crocodile-like animals. Like the largest snakes alive today, *Titanoboa* was a constricting snake, which means it didn't kill its prey with venom. Instead, it used its rows of needle-sharp teeth to catch hold of its prey, then wrapped itself around its victim and slowly squeezed it to death in its powerful crushing coils, until the prey animal could no longer breathe.

TITANOBOA ▲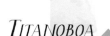

LIVED: 60 million years ago

SIZE: around 40 ft long, up to 3 ft thick

WEIGHT: 1 ton (or maybe more)

CREATURE FEATURE: giant-sized, needle-sharp teeth, and powerful, crushing coils

GREEN ANACONDA

The biggest snake alive today is the green anaconda, which also lives in South America. They live in a watery habitat— they're excellent swimmers! A green anaconda can reach 30 feet long, one foot thick, and weigh a hefty 550 pounds. Reticulated pythons, from Asia, can be even longer than anacondas, but aren't as heavy. These snakes are just babies compared to the humongous *Titanoboa*!

OPEN WIDE

Like snakes today, the *Titanoboa* had specially hinged jaws that could open incredibly wide to swallow large prey whole. The digestion process could take months, depending on the size of the animal.

GREEN ANACONDA ▼

40 ft

KOOLASUCHUS

Koolasuchus was like a carnivorous tadpole the size of a very big crocodile, and with a similar appetite. This huge flesh-eating creature lurked in watery habitats during the time of the dinosaurs.

KOOLASUCHUS ▲

SHOVEL HEAD

Koolasuchus was a very large amphibian. Its eyes were close to the top of its huge, shovel-shaped head, perfect for lying submerged in water waiting for prey to pass by (as crocodiles do today). *Koolasuchus* hunted fish, crabs, small dinosaurs, and reptiles in what's now South Australia. One hundred million years ago, that land mass was much closer to the South Pole, covered in thick forest, and icy cold and frozen for parts of the year, though there was no permanent snow. *Koolasuchus* probably hibernated at the coldest times.

LIVED: 137 to 112 million years ago
SIZE: 13 to 16 ft long

WEIGHT: up to 1000 lbs
CREATURE FEATURE:
a hundred huge, sharp teeth

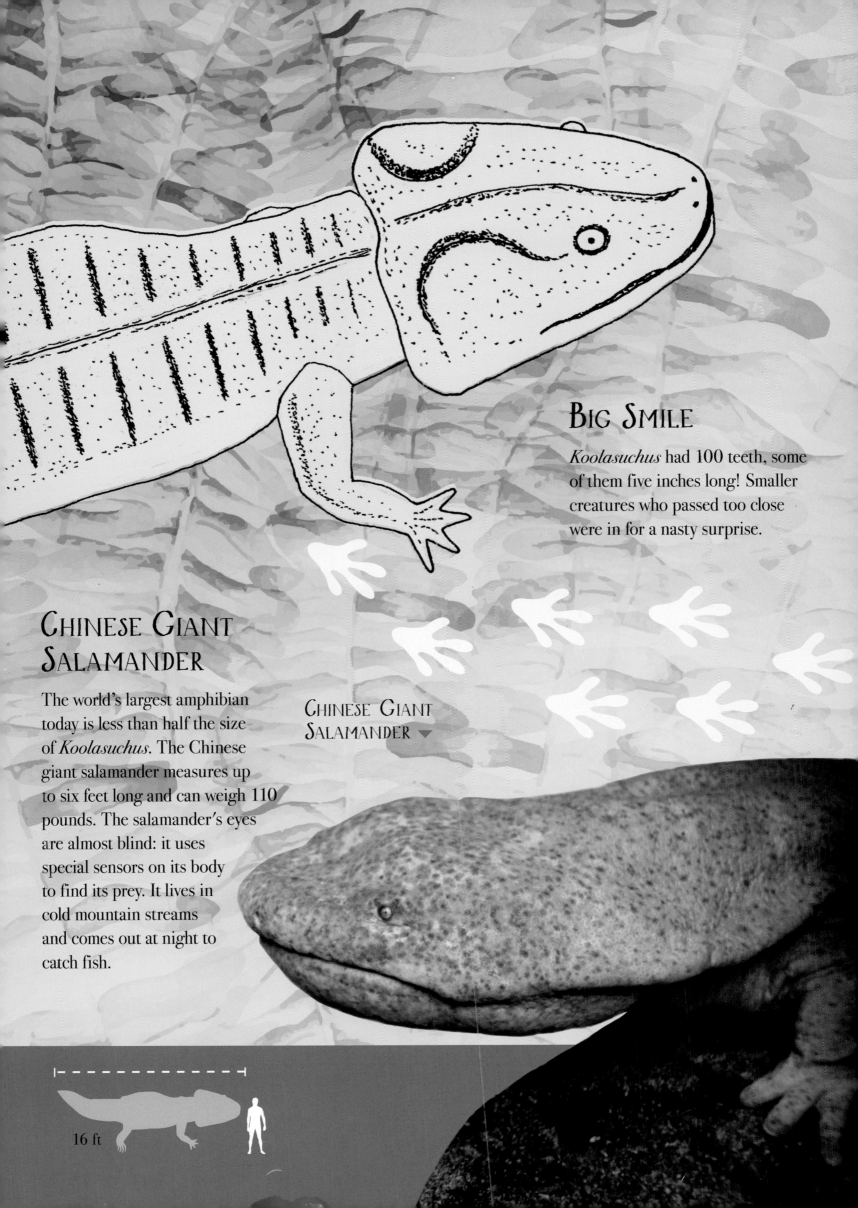

BIG SMILE

Koolasuchus had 100 teeth, some of them five inches long! Smaller creatures who passed too close were in for a nasty surprise.

CHINESE GIANT SALAMANDER

The world's largest amphibian today is less than half the size of *Koolasuchus*. The Chinese giant salamander measures up to six feet long and can weigh 110 pounds. The salamander's eyes are almost blind: it uses special sensors on its body to find its prey. It lives in cold mountain streams and comes out at night to catch fish.

CHINESE GIANT SALAMANDER ▼

16 ft

BRONTORNIS

These giant, flightless, flesh-eating birds would have been tall enough to peer into a second-floor bedroom window!

▲ *BRONTORNIS*

But don't worry, they terrorized South America long before people existed. They were some of the biggest birds ever.

LIVED: 6 million years ago
SIZE: 10 ft tall

WEIGHT: up to 900 lbs
CREATURE FEATURE: sharp beak and talons

Terror Birds

Brontornis is one of a group of meat-eating flightless birds called phorusrhacids, or terror birds. They were some of the top predators of their time, and probably the biggest. They had deadly, razor-sharp claws on their feet and savage, hatchet-shaped beaks. Because of its size, *Brontornis* probably wasn't a very fast runner and instead made ambush attacks on its prey. It was also too heavy to fly: its small, stubby wings were left over from its distant ancestors, which *could* fly.

Biggest Birds

Even the bulky *Brontornis* isn't the biggest bird ever—the elephant bird is the largest that's ever been discovered. They were more than ten feet tall, weighed up to 1,000 pounds, and lived until about 300 years ago on the island of Madagascar.

Feisty Ostrich

The largest bird alive today is the ostrich. It can't fly, but it can run astonishingly fast—up to 43 miles an hour. It can measure up to nine feet tall, and it has a long claw on its foot that can easily disembowel a large mammal—it's been suggested that *Brontornis* might have used a similar tactic to kill its prey. Ostrich eggs (also the largest in the world, not surprisingly!) measure on average six inches in length and can weigh three pounds.

OSTRICH ▶

10 ft

GIANT SHORT-FACED BEAR

The largest bear that ever lived, and also one of the biggest meat-eating mammals, this huge animal roamed the grasslands of South America. It fed on giant armadillos and other large animals as well as plants, and it intimidated packs of wolves and saber-toothed cats.

GIANT SHORT-FACED BEAR ▶

LIVED: 1.8 million to 500,000 years ago

SIZE: 12 feet (standing upright)

WEIGHT: 3500 lbs (though estimates vary)

CREATURE FEATURE: huge size, and the teeth and claws of a successful hunter

GREAT BEAR

Giant short-faced bears had longer legs than today's bears, so they would have been able to run fast–some scientists reckon as much as 40 miles an hour. However, the bear's massive weight meant that its legs couldn't support its body to run for very long. It hunted some, but it most likely got most of its food by scavenging the carcasses of other animals' prey. These bears were solitary animals, living on their own unless they were mothers with cubs.

BIG BROTHER

The largest bear alive today is the polar bear, but the giant short-faced bear was three feet taller and probably about twice as heavy!

SPECTACLED BEAR

The giant short-faced bear's closest living relative is the spectacled bear, which is South America's only bear. It's unlike its ancient ancestor in some ways: it's almost exclusively vegetarian, and it's much smaller–five feet tall and 330 pounds in weight. The spectacled bear gets its name from the yellow markings around its eyes.

SPECTACLED BEAR ▾

5 ft

ENTELODON

These scary-looking beasts may be distantly related to pigs, and they do look a bit like them—but monster killer ones! They were huge and aggressive, and roamed Europe and Asia millions of years ago.

TERRIBLE PIGS

Entelodons were as tall as an adult human, with massive heads around two feet long. Their giant jaws contained powerful ripping and grinding teeth. It's thought they ate just about anything—plants as well as meat—and they probably scavenged dead animals as well as hunting live ones. They were big enough to bring down prey the size of a cow, though they weren't especially fast.

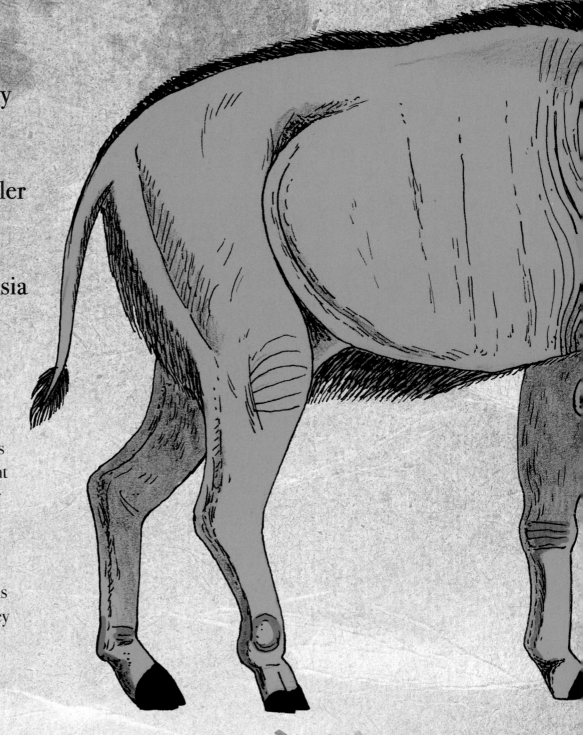

LIVED: 37 to 33 million years ago
SIZE: 5 ft tall at the shoulder

WEIGHT: 1 ton
CREATURE FEATURE: enormous, 2-foot-long head

▲ *Entelodon*

Food Fights

Entelodons were always up for a fight: many of their fossil skeletons show horrible wounds caused by other *Entelodons*. They might have fought over food or mating rights.

Giant Forest Hog

The biggest wild pig species today is the giant forest hog, which lives in central Africa. The biggest can grow to be seven feet long and weigh 600 pounds—though domestic pigs, bred for their meat, can grow even bigger. Giant forest hogs can be dangerous, especially when they have young hogs to protect—they have very sharp tusks.

Giant forest hog ▼

5 ft

QUETZALCOATLUS

Imagine a huge flying lizard the size of a small aircraft, with an enormous sharp, pointed beak . . . duck!

WHAT'S IN A NAME?

Quetzalcoatlus is named after Quetzalcoatl, the feathered snake god of Aztec mythology.

FLYING LIZARDS

Flying reptiles called "pterosaurs" were the first animals to fly, apart from insects. Each of their lizard hands had evolved an extremely long finger, which supported the animal's leathery wings. These creatures ruled the skies in the time of the dinosaurs. Some of them were very small, but *Quetzalcoatlus* was one of the biggest. If it flew at all, it loomed over North America, probably gliding more than flying. No one is sure how it fed: it might have scavenged meat from dead dinosaurs or speared small land animals with its sharp beak. Dinosaur experts used to think it caught fish in the sea, until they discovered that it lived hundreds of miles from the ocean!

LIVED: 70 to 66 million years ago

SIZE: wingspan up to 40 ft (estimates vary)

WEIGHT: around 500 lbs (estimates vary)

CREATURE FEATURE: enormous wingspan and long, pointed beak

◄ *QUETZALCOATLUS*

WANDERING ALBATROSS

This beautiful sea bird has the largest wingspan of any bird in the world today—up to 11 feet. These huge wings allow the bird to fly 600 miles in just one day. The birds can spend years flying across the sea without coming to land at all.

LAND ANIMAL?

Quetzalcoatlus was so big that it must have been difficult for it to take off. It might have used both its wings and its legs to push itself into the air. It has even been suggested that it never flew at all: some scientists think that the folded-up wings could have been used to walk about on all fours.

WANDERING ALBATROSS

40 ft

77

PREHISTORIC CREEPY-CRAWLIES

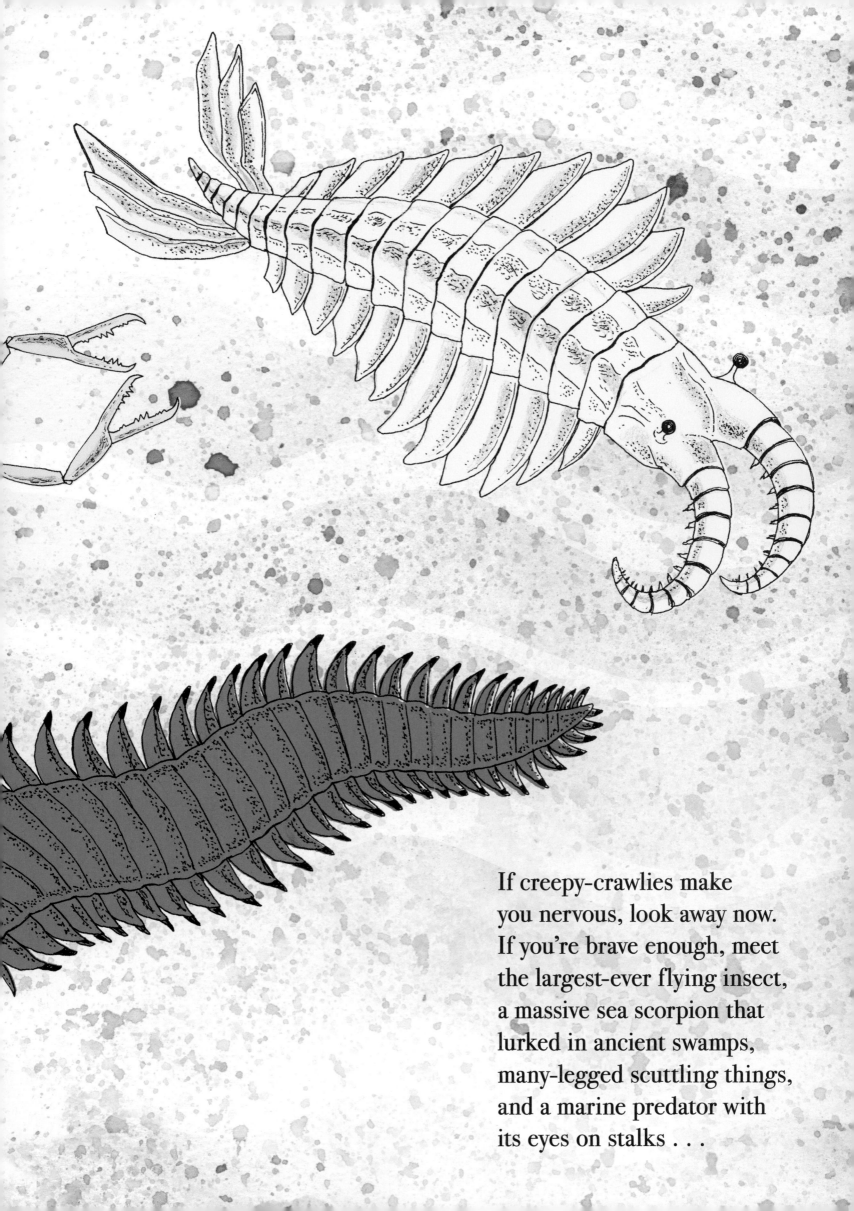

If creepy-crawlies make you nervous, look away now. If you're brave enough, meet the largest-ever flying insect, a massive sea scorpion that lurked in ancient swamps, many-legged scuttling things, and a marine predator with its eyes on stalks . . .

MEGANEURA

If you've ever waved a wasp away from your picnic sandwiches, imagine being bombarded by flying insects the size of a hawk. The dragonfly-like *Meganeura* is, as far as we know, the world's biggest-ever insect.

MEGANEURA ▶

WINGED HUNTER

Meganeura hunted other insects in tropical forests many millions of years ago in the time before the dinosaurs. It could swoop onto its prey quickly and with deadly accuracy, thanks to its two pairs of wings and excellent eyesight, then kill and eat it with powerful biting mouth parts. The larvae of *Meganeura*, like the larvae of modern dragonflies, were also fierce predators. They lived in swampy burrows and came out to find prey, which they dragged back to the burrow to devour.

LIVED: 310 to 280 million years ago

SIZE: wingspan up to 2.5 ft

WEIGHT: nearly 1 lb

CREATURE FEATURE: giant-sized, eagle-eyed, with 2 pairs of wings for aerial maneuvers

INSECT SUCCESS STORY

The oldest fossilized insects are 400 million years old, which is about when flying insects first appeared on the earth. Today, insects make up 95 percent of life on land.

DRAGONFLIES

Modern dragonflies have two pairs of wings and can beat each of them at different speeds and angles. They use them for complicated aerial acrobatics, just as *Meganeura* must have done. They can fly in any direction—even backwards—and hover for up to a minute. The biggest measured wingspan of any modern dragonfly or damselfly is over seven inches.

DRAGONFLY

2.5 ft

JAEKELOPTERUS

Arthropods are the animal group that includes insects, crabs, lobsters, spiders, and scorpions. You're about to meet the biggest one that ever lived . . .

SEA SCORPION

Jaekelopterus was a huge sea scorpion. Its giant body, longer than a tall man's, was too big and heavy to move on land: it lived submerged in coastal swamps, lakes, and rivers around 390 million years ago. We know about *Jaekelopterus* because a fossil claw, 18 inches long, was discovered in Germany—the giant claw was armed with sharp spikes for gripping the slippery fish and other sea creatures it preyed on. It was the top water predator of its time, and as well as eating fishy prey it also cannibalized other *Jaekelopteri*. There were other, smaller kinds of sea scorpion that crawled up onto land to shed their outer skins or mate. Although it's known as a sea scorpion, it probably spent most of its time in fresh water.

JAEKELOPTERUS

LIVED: 390 to 250 million years ago

SIZE: 8 ft long

WEIGHT: possibly up to 90 lbs

CREATURE FEATURE: huge spiked claws

Spider Crab

Today's biggest arthropod is the Japanese spider crab, which spends all its time in deep, cold seas. A Japanese spider crab can live to be 100 years old! It isn't as big as *Jaekelopterus*, but its long, thin legs can span 12 feet. A spider crab will adorn itself with sponges and algae to help hide from predators (such as octopi).

Emperor Scorpion

Emperor scorpions are some of the biggest scorpions alive today. They can measure eight inches long and have gigantic claws. Although they look very scary, they're actually quite shy creatures, and their venom isn't very dangerous to people.

8 ft

ARTHROPLEURA

The millipede of your darkest dreams, many-legged *Arthropleura* scuttled across Carboniferous forests more than two hundred million years ago.

BIG BUGS

Arthropleura was an arthropod, like *Jaekelopterus*. It's the biggest land arthropod that's ever been discovered, at more than eight feet long. All those legs carried *Arthropleura* quickly across the forest floor as it looked for food. The creature's mouthparts have never been found, but they probably ate plants as modern millipedes do. Amazingly, you can still see *Arthropleura*'s footprints today— the creature's multi-legged tracks have become fossilized in rocks in different parts of the world.

ARTHROPLEURA ▶

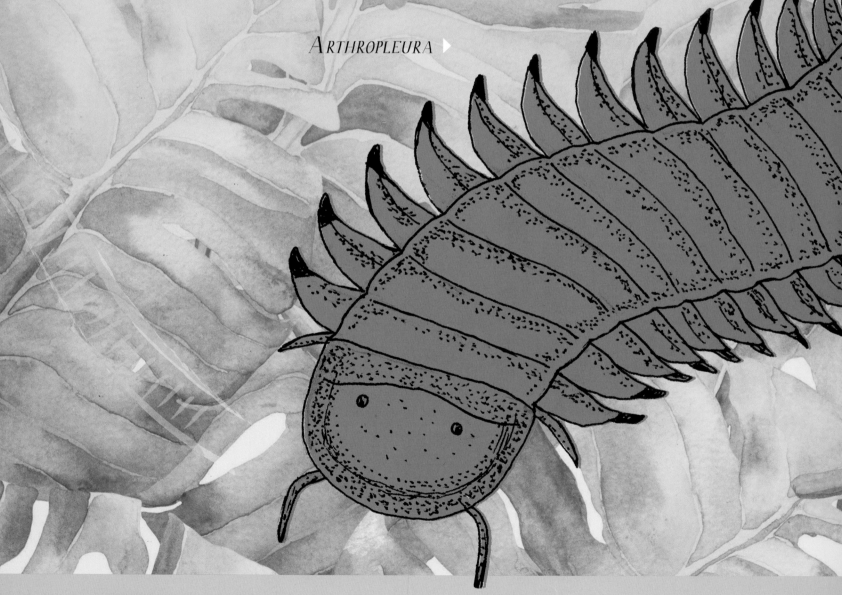

LIVED: 340 to 280 million years ago
SIZE: up to 8 ft long

WEIGHT: we can't be sure!
CREATURE FEATURE: many legs

First to Land

The first creatures to crawl out of the sea and on to land weren't our relatives (which were fish that evolved stumpy legs). The first land animals were also arthropods, though not nearly as big as *Arthropleura*.

Millipedes

Millipedes are alive and well today, and the longest, the giant African millipede, can measure up to 12 inches. Millipede means "a thousand legs," but they don't really have that many—most have fewer than 100. The record-holder is a Californian underground millipede that has 750! Millipedes have only three pairs of legs when they hatch. A millipede adds more body segments (and legs) every time it moults.

MILLIPEDE ▼

8 ft

ANOMALOCARIS

This ancient marine predator must have been a terrifying sight 520 million years ago, when it was the biggest creature alive. It was ten times the size of any other animal of its time that's been discovered so far—and it had a big mouth ringed with sharp plates.

UNUSUAL ARTHROPOD

Anomalocaris was an arthropod, like *Jaekelopterus* and *Arthropleura* (pages 82 and 84). Like lots of modern arthropods, *Anomalocaris* was a meat-eater and had a segmented body. But it had lots of differences too: it swam by moving the flaps on its sides up and down, and it had large eyes on stalks and a mouth underneath its head containing sharp plates for slicing its prey. Some scientists wonder if it's an arthropod at all!

ANOMALOCARIS ▲

Anomalocaris fossils have been found worldwide!

LIVED: 535 to 520 million years ago

SIZE: up to 6 ft long

WEIGHT: up to 20 lbs

CREATURE FEATURE: eyes on stalks, snapping jaws, and strange side flaps

▲ GIANT ISOPOD

GIANT ISOPODS

Giant isopods are some of today's strangest arthropods. They're like giant marine woodlice, but quite a bit uglier. They measure up to 14 inches long, have four sets of jaws, and are found on the deep seafloor, where they feed on dead animals and plants.

FOSSIL CLUES

Trilobites were common when *Anomalocaris* ruled the seas. Their fossils have been found with a wedge-shaped bite taken out of their shells, which may have been made by the sharp mouthparts of *Anomalocaris*.

6 ft

PREHISTORIC TIMELINE

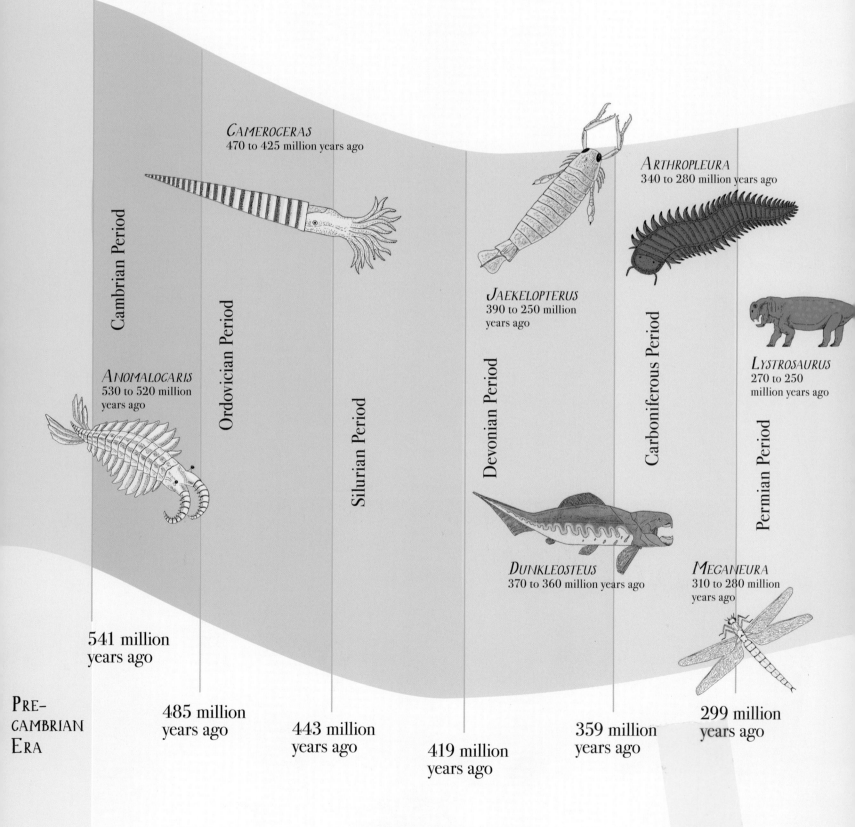

CAMEROCERAS
470 to 425 million years ago

ARTHROPLEURA
340 to 280 million years ago

JAEKELOPTERUS
390 to 250 million
years ago

LYSTROSAURUS
270 to 250
million years ago

Cambrian Period

Ordovician Period

Silurian Period

Devonian Period

Carboniferous Period

Permian Period

ANOMALOCARIS
530 to 520 million
years ago

DUNKLEOSTEUS
370 to 360 million years ago

MEGANEURA
310 to 280 million
years ago

541 million
years ago

PRE-
CAMBRIAN
ERA

485 million
years ago

443 million
years ago

419 million
years ago

359 million
years ago

299 million
years ago

PALEOZOIC ERA

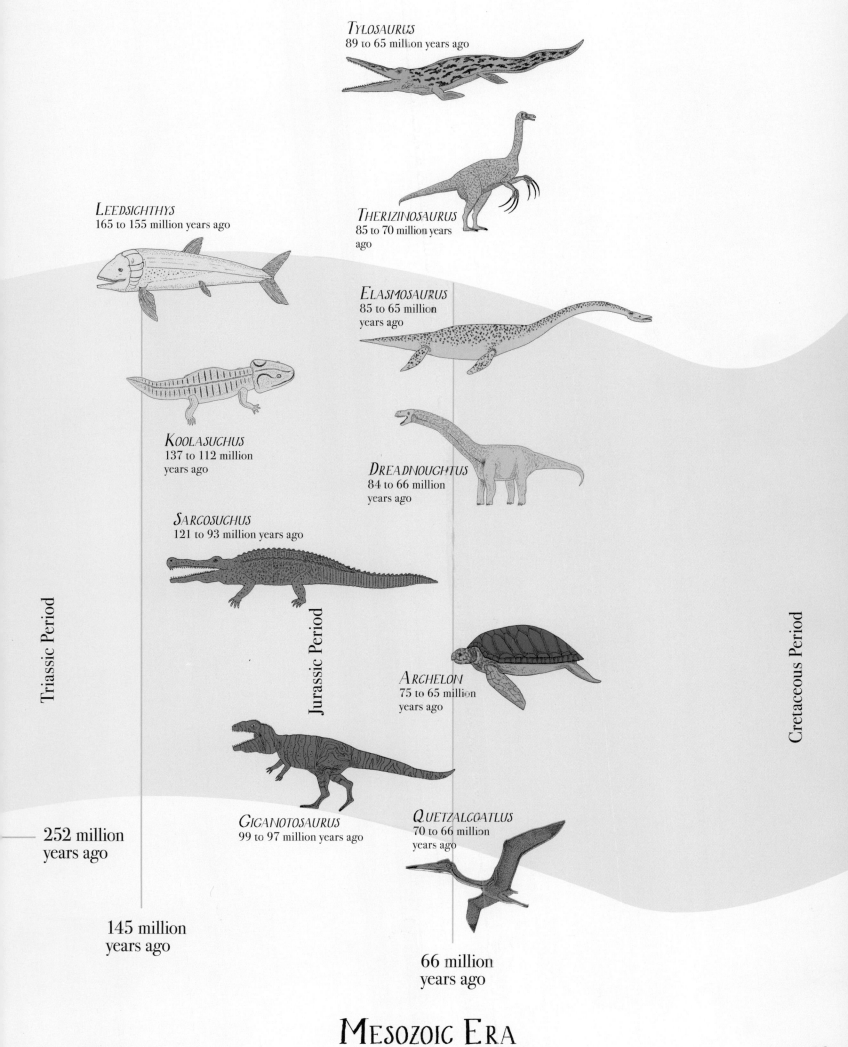

Tylosaurus
89 to 65 million years ago

Therizinosaurus
85 to 70 million years ago

Leedsichthys
165 to 155 million years ago

Elasmosaurus
85 to 65 million years ago

Koolasuchus
137 to 112 million years ago

Dreadnoughtus
84 to 66 million years ago

Sarcosuchus
121 to 93 million years ago

Archelon
75 to 65 million years ago

Triassic Period

Jurassic Period

Cretaceous Period

Giganotosaurus
99 to 97 million years ago

Quetzalcoatlus
70 to 66 million years ago

252 million years ago

145 million years ago

66 million years ago

Mesozoic Era

TITANOBOA
60 million years ago

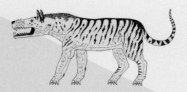

UINTATHERIUM
50 to 37 million years ago

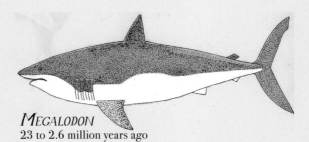

MEGALODON
23 to 2.6 million years ago

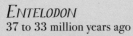

ANDREWSARCHUS
40 to 35 million years ago

EPIGAULUS
16 to 5 million
years ago

ENTELODON
37 to 33 million years ago

ARSINOITHERIUM
36 to 30 million years ago

GIGANTOPITHECUS
9 million to 100,000
years ago

Palaogene Period

Neogene Period

PARACERATHERIUM
30 to 25 million years ago

BRONTORNIS
6 million years ago

CHALICOTHERIUM
28 to 5 million
years ago

— 66 million
years ago

23 million
years ago

GIANT PACARANA
4 to 2 million years ago

SMILODON
2.5 million to 10,000
years ago

MEGATHERIUM
1.9 million to
8,000 years ago

DOEDICURUS
2 million to 11,000
years ago

GIANT SHORT-FACED BEAR
1.8 million to 500,000 years ago

WOOLLY RHINOCEROS
350,000 to 10,000 years
ago

GIANT KANGAROO
300,000 to 50,000
years ago

WOOLLY MAMMOTH
120,000 to 10,000 years ago

HOMO SAPIENS
120,000 years ago

IRISH ELK
100,000 to 7,000
years ago

Quaternary Period

Toward the
present . . .

—— 2.5 million
years ago

CENOZOIC ERA

GLOSSARY

ambush a surprise attack

ammonite a type of mollusc that is now extinct

amphibians the animal group that includes frogs, toads, and salamanders; amphibians live both in water and on land, and lay their eggs in water

arthropods the animal group that includes insects, crabs, lobsters, spiders, and scorpions; arthropods have jointed legs and skeletons on the outside of their bodies

bacteria living things that are made up of just one cell and can sometimes cause diseases

canine a pointed tooth, often larger in meat eaters

cartilage tough tissue that connects joints and bones in the human body and makes up the skeletons of some fish, including sharks

critically endangered very much in danger of dying out and becoming extinct

disembowel split open and remove the internal organs

evolution the process by which living organisms gradually develop over a very long period of time, to help them survive better in their habitat

extinct when something has died out completely

fawn baby deer

frostbite damage caused to body tissue due to freezing

genes instructions in the cells of a living thing that provide all the information about its characteristics

grinding crushing or wearing down

jet propulsion releasing a fast-moving jet of liquid or gas backward in order to move forward

keratin a type of protein found in skin, nails, claws, hooves, teeth, and hair

mangrove swampy forest growing on a tropical coast

migration when animals make a long journey from one area to another at certain times of the year

petrified turned into stone

plain a large, flat area of land

plankton tiny plants and animals that float around freely in seawater

predator an animal that hunts and eats other animals

preserved when something is kept in its original state and has not decayed

prey an animal that is hunted and eaten by other animals

pterosaurs flying reptiles that lived at the same time as dinosaurs

rodent the mammal group that includes squirrels, hamsters, and mice; rodents have teeth that never stop growing

scavenging feeding on dead animals that other animals have killed

segmented made up of parts, or segments

solitary living alone, rather than with others

submerged completely under water

termite ant-like insect that lives in large groups and builds complex nests

trilobite a hard-shelled, segmented sea creature that is now extinct

vegetarian an animal or person that does not eat meat

venom a poisonous substance that a creature injects into its prey or enemies

venomous able to inject venom using a sting, fangs, or spines

vertebrae small bones that make up the spine

wade walk through water

INDEX